Cryptocurrency

The Prominence Of Dash Digital Currency As The Cryptocurrency Of The Future And Strategies To Capitalize On Its Profitable Potential

(An In-Depth Handbook On Bitcoin Trading And Altcoin Trading)

FRANCIS DODD

TABLE OF CONTENT

Introduction

Cryptocurrencies have made significant advancements in a relatively brief period. They have observed a recurring pattern of ascent, decline, and reemergence. If you are an early cryptocurrency adopter, you would acknowledge that the path has been exceedingly tumultuous.

Similar to various facets of existence, the ascent and descent of digital currencies have not been devoid of divergent perspectives. The concept of cryptocurrency holds great intrigue for certain individuals, while for others, it elicits disinterest. For the remaining individuals, this idea is perplexing. On one side, there are individuals with an optimistic outlook who believe that cryptocurrencies represent the future trajectory. On the opposite end of the spectrum are individuals who possess a

1

pessimistic view and disregard them as a passing trend in the digital realm.

Nevertheless, regardless of whether you are an impartial individual desiring to engage in the cryptocurrency industry or an individual who has already developed a stance concerning cryptocurrencies and their underlying technology, this book will provide you with comprehensive insights to help you comprehend all the essential aspects of digital currencies. By doing so, it will enable you to make decisions with enhanced knowledge and understanding.

What would be the recommended method for purchasing Bitcoin within your nation?

Globally, local bitcoins, BitSquare, and Bitcoin ATMs are viable options for cryptocurrency transactions in virtually any location worldwide. While these alternatives are indeed feasible, it is advisable to explore additional possibilities that are accessible within your local area.

NORTH AMERICA

The United States and Canada are widely recognized as prominent Bitcoin markets. Buyers have the option to acquire Bitcoins through various means. In addition to LocalBitcoins and ATMs, there are also direct vendors such as Coinbase, Circle, India Coin, the P2P-market Paxful, and the exchange Kraken that can be accessed in both countries.

The nation of the United States of America.

• Peer-to-Peer Transactions: Coinbase and Kraken, prominent platforms in the cryptocurrency market, facilitate the seamless purchase of Bitcoins at minimal transaction costs while enabling users to securely store their digital assets in an online wallet. Both services are compatible with both credit cards and bank transfers. Indacoin represents an alternative direct exchange system; however, it is devoid of an integrated wallet feature. In addition, Expresscoin provides the capability to purchase Bitcoins with physical currency through the utilization of Billpay.

• P2P Platforms: Apart from LocalBitcoins and Bitsquare, consumers in the United States can also access P2P platforms such as Bitquick and Paxful. When utilizing Bitquick, payment is facilitated through cash deposits into the seller's designated bank account. In contrast, Paxful offers the seller a plethora of payment options to choose from, encompassing PayPal, Western Union, credit and debit cards, gift cards, and an assortment of additional alternatives. Despite the typically elevated rates on Paxful, Bitquick implements a 2% fee.

• Cryptocurrency Exchanges: Several reputable platforms offer the option to purchase Bitcoins using US Dollars on a digital asset exchange. The most prevalent exchanges, in chronological order, are Bitstamp, GDAX (owned by Coinbase), and Bitfinex. Subsequently, BTC-E, Kraken, and Gemini also rank among commonly utilized platforms. While the majority of exchanges solely facilitate bank transfers, BTC-E offers users the option to fund their accounts through alternative means, including credit cards and various payment providers such as PerfectMoney, Paysafecards, and similar options.

CANADA

• Kraken and Coinbase both cater to customers in Canada, offering them the ability to buy Bitcoins through bank transfers or credit cards and subsequently store them in the platforms' online wallets. Indacoin is accessible to customers hailing from Canada as well. For instance, QuickBT and canadianbitcoins.com are online platforms that enable individuals to procure Bitcoins directly by making payments of up to 150 Canadian Dollars, employing diverse payment modes like INTERAC® Online and Flexepin Vouchers. Cash payments in person or through deposit are also accepted by Canadianbitcoin.com.

•Peer-to-Peer: Canadian customers have the option to acquire Bitcoins from international peer-to-peer markets such as Paxful and LocalBitcoin.

•Trading: There are available markets where Canadian Dollars can be traded. Kraken and CoinSquare are widely recognized as the most prominent instances.

Latin America

With the exception of North America, the adoption of Bitcoins in Middle and South America commenced only in the years 2014 and 2015. Due to the limited trading activity and liquidity, investors are compelled to incur higher fees and spreads on most recent transactions.

Satoshi Tango serves as an authorized distributor in a number of South and Middle American countries, namely Brazil, Chile, Colombia, Costa Rica, Ecuador, El Salvador, Guatemala, Honduras, Mexico, Nicaragua, Panama, and Peru, operating under the name Bitex. L&A serves as a direct supplier for the markets in Argentina, Chile, Colombia, and Uruguay.

Local bitcoins can be found on the peer-to-peer market in a majority of Latin American nations.

MEXICO

• Bitcoin Gift Cards: The Chip-Chap.com app offers the convenient option to buy

Bitcoin gift cards from more than 5,000 stores.

• Indirect: Volabit.com offers users the opportunity to acquire Bitcoin using Mexican Pesos (MXN) by means of bank transfers or by making cash deposits at various locations such as OXXO, 7-Eleven, Banamex branches, and ATMs.

•Trading Platform: Bitso.com operates as a renowned exchange based in Mexico. The fees exhibit a consistent decline in tandem with the growth in trade volume, reaching as minimal as 0.1 percent, while the spread remains negligible in size.

BRAZIL

• In a straightforward manner: Brazilian individuals have the option to make direct purchases of Bitcoins through Mercadobitcoin.com.br, a brokerage firm that asserts itself as the largest Bitcoin exchange in Latin America.

• Major Bitcoin exchanges in Brazil include FlowBTC. Bitcoin transactions can be conducted on this platform. The utilization of ban on transfers may serve the purpose of making deposits. Foxbit.com.br is a prominent secondary cryptocurrency exchange.

ARGENTINA

•Indirect: The Ripio wallet application facilitates the acquisition of Bitcoins for users. Its distinguishing characteristic lies in its ability to facilitate the purchase of Bitcoins on credit while serving as a conduit for Bitcoin transactions.

In the country of Venezuela, it is possible to acquire Bitcoin.

• Bitcoin exchange: SurBitcoin operates as Venezuela's native Bitcoin exchange platform.

CHILE

•Cryptocurrency Trading Platform: Chile is home to SurBTC, a renowned Bitcoin trading platform that garnered global attention following its endorsement by the government. Bitcoins are available for purchase and sale on this platform, and individuals have the option to deposit Chilean pesos using local bank transfers.

EUROPE

•Automated Teller Machines (ATMs): The website coinatmradar.com provides a comprehensive compilation of numerous Bitcoin ATMs situated across Europe.

• Indirect: Owing to the ambiguous regulatory landscape in the Eurozone, an abundance of Bitcoin exchanges exist that facilitate transactions with various forms of payment. The majority of these brokers levy fees ranging from 0.5% to 5% on their customers, which vary according to the payment channel utilized and derive profit from the spread. Although the aforementioned platforms solely facilitate the purchase of Bitcoin and lack a sophisticated web-based wallet, Coinbase and Circle offer an online wallet equipped with features enabling the acquisition of Bitcoin through bank transfers or credit card payment methods in a majority of European nations.

•P2P Markets: With the exception of Germany, LocalBitcoin is accessible in all Eurozone countries apart from Germany. Bitcoin.de serves as a peer-to-peer (P2P) platform catering to the entire Eurozone, facilitating the purchase and sale of Bitcoins through SEPA transfers. Apart from cryptocurrency exchanges, Bitcoin.de offers the most cost-effective method for acquiring Bitcoins, boasting a nominal 0.5% commission rate and a favorable spread.

•Currency exchange: Certain currency exchanges cater specifically to the Eurozone. The predominant cryptocurrency exchange is Kraken, which is subsequently pursued by Bitstamp and BTC-E. All transactions necessitate complete Know Your Customer (KYC) verification.

AUSTRIA,

Gift vouchers originating from bitcoin. Austrian citizens have the option to utilize the services of various traffic shops to acquire At, which can then be employed for the purpose of purchasing Bitcoins. This method juxtaposes convenience with a higher cost, making it the most favorable option for acquiring Bitcoins.

THE GERMANS

The Fidor-Bank presents a favorable opportunity for German individuals to initiate their acquisition of Bitcoins. These online banks have established strategic alliances with Bitcoin.de and Kraken to enhance the efficiency and convenience of trading on said platforms. Fidor customers will immediately gain full Know Your Customer (KYC) status and swiftly utilize the ExpressTrade feature on Bitcoin.de. This grants them the ability to acquire an unlimited quantity of Bitcoins at competitive rates promptly upon reaching out to the website.

SPAIN

By utilizing the services of Bit2Me.com and chip-chap.com, it is possible to acquire Bitcoins from a multitude of ATMs located throughout Spain.

EUROPE

Localbitcoins can be accessed in nearly all European countries. Due to the advantageous exchange rate existing between local currencies and the Euro, numerous European nations engage in the acquisition of Bitcoins via prominent

European platforms such as Kraken and bitcoin.de. Due to the substantial surcharges imposed by small exchanges and their wide availability, the resulting premium on prices can be significant. Consequently, opting to convert the local currency to Euro and utilizing Euro-based platforms, which generally cater to clients from across Europe, often proves to be a more economical approach.

If a credit card is at one's disposal, it serves as a convenient means of payment. The credit card issuer derives financial gain from the differential in currency exchange rates and fees; nonetheless, you have the option to expediently and conveniently acquire Bitcoins.

What is Ethereum?

Ethereum was created in 2015 by Vitali Buterin and functions as a cryptocurrency offering ether tokens.

This is equivalent to the bitcoins present within the Bitcoin network. Ethereum is employed for the development and transmission of decentralized applications with their backend code residing in a distributed, peer-to-peer network. This differs from a typical application in which the back-end code is integrated into a consolidated server. Ether is also employed as remuneration for services rendered, such as the computational resources required prior to the inclusion of a block in the blockchain, as well as transaction fees.

Ethereum functions similarly to Bitcoin and can be leveraged for decentralized payments. Similarly, the utilization of smart contracts can be employed. Smart contracts operate in a manner where the fulfillment of a specific arrangement comprising pre-established regulations leads to the occurrence of a predetermined outcome.

Bitcoin versus Ethereum

The debate surrounding the comparison between Bitcoin and Ethereum has garnered increasing attention in recent times. Bitcoin has gained widespread recognition and acclaim as a prominent and globally recognized digital currency. Furthermore, it possesses the highest market capitalization among all the cryptocurrencies currently available. Indeed, it currently holds the prestigious title in the realm of cryptocurrencies. On the contrary, however, Ethereum is situated. Ethereum did not possess the same progressive influence as Bitcoin; nonetheless, its creator leveraged insights from Bitcoin to develop additional functionalities that were built upon the principles of Bitcoin. It currently ranks as the second most prominent digital currency in existence.

4. Decentralized Applications (Dapps)

May we draw a distinction between decentralized applications and conventional applications? Upon logging into Twitter, an instance of a web application is presented, which is constructed using HTML, as a prime example. When you sign in to Twitter, as an illustration, a web application is displayed that is constructed using HTML. The webpage will utilize a Programming connection point to access and manipulate your data, which has already undergone substantial processing. It entails a distinct partnership: your front-end effectively implements the back-end programming interface, while the programming connection point seamlessly retrieves your data from a centralized database.

When we transition this application into a decentralized application, a comparative web application is deployed upon signing in. However, it makes use of a smart contract-based programming interface to retrieve data from the blockchain network. In this regard, the utilization of a sophisticated contract interface serves to supplant the Programming point of interaction, and the intelligent comprehension will facilitate the retrieval of information from the underlying blockchain network.

That blockchain network is unequivocally not a centralized database; rather, it operates as a decentralized organization wherein the members of the association (the validators) authenticate every transaction taking place through the implementation of smart contracts on the blockchain network. As a result, any trade or transaction occurring on a Twitter-like platform that has undergone modification will be classified as a decentralized trade.

A decentralized application (Dapp) comprises a sponsorship code that unpredictably amplifies demand within a network characterized by distributed communication. It is an object anticipated to function within the

Ethereum network autonomously, as specified, and that is the fundamental distinction: it facilitates direct connectivity between end-users and decentralized application providers.

A Dapp is deemed eligible when it meets the criteria of being open-source (with its code publicly available on Github) and utilizes a token based on a public blockchain to execute its operations. A representative acts as the energy source necessary for the decentralized application to function. Dapp facilitates the decentralization of the back-end code and data through licensing, constituting a core tenet of any Dapp's overarching strategy.

5. Decentralized Autonomous Organizations (DAOs)

A DAO is an electronic organization that operates autonomously, without the need for central control or a reliance on network latency. It functions in a decentralized manner, relying on ubiquity-based principles. In essence, a

DAO can be described as an organization in which the leadership is not centralized, but ideally lies in the hands of designated experts or a group of assigned individuals, constituting a form of distributed authority. It is present within a blockchain network, wherein it is referenced by the manifestations incorporated within a smart contract. Consequently, decentralized autonomous organizations depend on intelligent mechanisms for navigating, which can be likened to decentralized voting systems within the organization. In a similar vein, prior to making any subsequent determination, it is imperative that the democratic process is followed, which operates on a decentralized application.

This secret has been meticulously monitored. Individuals contribute resources to the DAO in accordance with the manner by which the DAO anticipates securing funding and making decisions. Given the aforementioned circumstances, each component is assigned a representative who is entrusted with handling the corresponding individual's share of contributions within the DAO. The tokens serve the purpose of projecting a polling form within the DAO, with the evaluation of the recommendation status being determined based on the most favorable votes. All decisions within the organization must undergo this formal balloting process.

Valid Applications of Ethereum

• Administering a survey-based software platform

As exemplified by the case of DAO, the adoption of a polling form system on the Ethereum network is becoming increasingly apparent. The outcomes of the investigations are fully transparent, thereby guaranteeing a transparent and equitable collaboration by eliminating any potential biased conduct in survey administration.

•Banking Systems

Ethereum is being widely adopted in financial systems due to its decentralized architecture, as it presents a deterrent to unauthorized access for developers. In addition, it facilitates transactions on a network built on the Ethereum platform. As a result, financial institutions are also incorporating Ethereum as a means of conducting payments and transactions.

•Conveying

Facilitating the transfer of Ethereum in transportation enhances the tracking of shipments and safeguards against the risk of loss or duplication of inventory. Ethereum provides the traceability and tracking framework for any asset anticipated within a conventional supply chain.

•Plans

With the utilization of Ethereum smart contract, plans can be effectively monitored and executed with minimal modification. Therefore, in an industry that segregates individuals, is likely to deliberate, and necessitates automated solutions to be present, Ethereum can be utilized as a breakthrough for constructing smart contracts and securely managing the agreements and transactions associated with them.

Technical Analysis

Technical analysis, often abbreviated as TA, employs historical data to anticipate forthcoming cryptocurrency prices and market trends. It aims to forecast whether the price trends will ascend (bullish) or descend (bearish). This is achieved by utilizing technical indicators, which evaluate the past and present market value of an asset and scrutinize patterns in price fluctuations.

The assessment of historical price charts alongside gathered volume data enables the determination of whether the coin is undervalued or overvalued.

Technical analysis is predicated upon the underlying assumptions outlined herein.

The pricing dynamics adhere to specific patterns. Bitcoin prices exhibit non-random behavior and show a tendency to adhere to specific patterns, which can persist for varying durations, be it short-term or long-term. It employs historical performance as a means of forecasting future prices.

The pricing of Bitcoin is influenced by various factors. The fluctuation in the value of the cryptocurrency is attributable to historical and anticipated demand for the coin, prevailing market rates, and the regulatory framework governing the cryptocurrency market.

Past events often have a tendency to recur. The events that have transpired in the previous occurrences serve as a predictive basis for future outcomes. Previous fluctuations can effectively anticipate forthcoming shifts in the market. Traders exhibit a tendency to act in a similar manner when confronted with comparable market conditions.

Classifications of Technical Analysis

Technical analysis utilizes three key components:

Graphical lines: Graphical lines serve the purpose of denoting the locations where changes in price occur. By utilizing historical price data, present prices, and volume data, analysts have the ability to plot charting lines that illustrate the precise junctures at which prices are inclined to shift.

Patterns: Chart patterns can be utilized to forecast fluctuations in price. They demonstrate the trajectory of prices and project future price movements.

Indicator oscillators: This analytical tool employs statistical techniques to ascertain the signals for buying and selling.

Chart analysis serves as a crucial tool for analysts and cryptocurrency investors alike, enabling them to efficiently obtain visual representations of price trends and market momentum.

Technical Indicators

Technical indicators are analytical instruments employed to compute and decipher market patterns in investment analysis. Traders depend on these instruments to ascertain the optimal moment for investment in cryptocurrencies. Investors have the capability to receive notifications regarding any emerging investment opportunities and fluctuations in prices.

Traders have the ability to discern the price fluctuations of cryptocurrency assets in various directions, namely upward, downward, or laterally. The calculation of price movement is derived from an analysis incorporating historical price data, prevailing prices, and data on trade volume.

Technical indicators play a vital role in the analysis of cryptocurrency investments. "They assist investors in: They aid investors in: They support investors in: They facilitate investors in: They enable investors to: They provide assistance to investors in: They offer guidance to investors in: They empower investors to: They contribute to the success of investors by: They play a role in assisting investors to: They serve as a resource for investors in: They collaborate with investors to: They work alongside investors to: They act as a partner to investors, helping them to:

Anticipate fluctuations in price and ascertain future price trends.

Validate the prevailing market patterns observed in the price fluctuations of digital currencies, notably Bitcoin.

Notify investors about the direction of prices, whether they are increasing, decreasing, or remaining stagnant, in order to enable traders to strategize and prepare for future trades.

Cryptocurrency investors depend on these indicators to ascertain the immediate price fluctuations. In addition, they assess the long-term fluctuations in the asset's pricing in order to ascertain the opportune moments for market entry or exit.

A few of the prevalent technical indicators employed entail the computation of Moving Averages (MA) and the determination of the Relative Strength Index (RSI). As an illustration, it is possible to create a graphical representation to demonstrate the trend of Bitcoin prices over the course of 12 and 26 days, correspondingly.

There are multiple factors to consider when examining a specific cryptocurrency asset. In order to select the appropriate indicator, it is imperative to possess a comprehensive comprehension of the functional mechanisms of each indicator, as well as their potential ramifications on your investment approach.

Due to the inherent volatility of cryptocurrency assets, closely observing the price trend or analyzing a graphical representation of Bitcoin's price fluctuations will enable investors to assess both the higher and lower trading patterns. Should the chart exhibit an upward trajectory, it would signify an escalation in trend lines, while a downward trajectory would indicate a succession of diminished trend lines.

On occasion, the cryptocurrency may exhibit a lateral movement. In such an occurrence, it remains stationary in the vertical axis devoid of any discernible movement. Investors are advised to exercise utmost caution when relying solely on a single indicator, such as trend lines, for the purpose of prognosticating future price movements, given that trends are susceptible to moving in a multitude of directions. It is significantly more advisable to rely on multiple indicators for the purpose of substantiating a directional movement, whether upward or downward.

A technical analysis chart is a graphical representation utilizing historical prices and trading volume data, depicting the past investment decisions pertaining to the buying and selling of cryptocurrency assets, as made by investors. As investors, we employ historical data to forecast forthcoming investment opportunities. As an illustration, an ordinary investor who has purchased Bitcoin will closely monitor the fluctuations in its price. Should the price decline in relation to the original purchase price, the investor may opt to hold their cryptocurrency until it achieves the break-even point before considering sale. As astute investors, we acknowledge this as Support/Resistance (elaborated further in this book) and can leverage this knowledge to our benefit.

Trend Analysis

Trend analysis employs technical indicators to ascertain price fluctuations, thereby aiding traders in making informed decisions regarding buying, selling, or retaining a cryptocurrency asset.

This methodology examines historical cryptocurrency prices in order to forecast future price fluctuations. It ascertains an ascending trajectory when the prices of assets persistently escalate, and identifies a descending trajectory when prices consistently decline for a series of consecutive days.

Trend lines, moving averages, and polarity analysis constitute the primary methodologies employed in ascertaining price trends. In the subsequent , our emphasis shall be directed towards the utilization of trend lines.

The utilization of trend lines represents a widely employed methodology within the realm of technical analysis. They serve to indicate the consistent fluctuation of prices in an upward, downward, or lateral direction. Price fluctuations differ, contingent upon the time frame and the type of observation undertaken by the investor, be it daily, weekly, monthly, or quarterly.

Drawing Trend Lines

Trend lines serve to depict the overall trajectory of the price. Lines are drawn horizontally above and below the price line. Trend lines additionally exhibit areas of support and resistance, thereby enabling the identification of opportune entry and exit points in a trading context. Trend lines have the potential to demonstrate an upward trajectory in supply or demand.

In formal tone: "Descending trend lines are positioned above the price of the plotted graph, whereas ascending trend lines are positioned beneath the price." The ascending trend line is employed for the purpose of approximating support, whereas the descending trendlines are utilized to gauge resistance.

Techniques for Sketching Trend Lines

Access the TradingView website and subsequently select the BTC/USD charts. This indicates the up-to-the-minute fluctuation in the value of Bitcoin, denominated in US Dollars.

One has the ability to personalize the chart and create trend lines upon it. To accomplish this task, please select the icon that represents a comprehensive chart, which will grant you access to an array of advanced chart tools for the purpose of customizing your chart.

One has the ability to modify the chart trend to encompass daily, weekly, or monthly intervals, subsequently deploying the available tools to delineate trend lines. Please choose the Trend Line Tool located on the left-hand side of the chart.

Trading Channels

A channel is comprised of a duo of linear segments, wherein one segment is positioned above the ascending trend line while the other segment is drawn parallel to the bottom, connecting the low points of a price series chart.

Channels are employed in the visualization of data in order to ascertain the ideal timing for the acquisition and divestment of cryptocurrency assets. The upper and lower boundaries are indicated to display the levels of support and resistance on the trading chart.

Trading channels provide insight into the potential points at which prices are expected to change direction. If an asset maintains its trading activity within the confines of two trend lines over a specific duration, it can be categorized as trading within the channel. If there is a consistent upward movement in the trading price, then it can be classified as an ascending channel. When the price exhibits a decline within the boundaries of the trend lines, it is denoted as a descending channel. When there is a lateral movement in the price, it gives rise to the formation of a horizontal channel.

The formation of the channel can be accomplished either by utilizing trend lines to delineate two lines, or by utilizing the channel tools that are accessible within the software.

Cryptocurrency Structure

The incorporation of Bitcoin enables the formation of a decentralized communication system among peers. As aforementioned, the idea is to avert server functions that have the potential to expand or be vulnerable to control by central authorities, governments, and other entities.

Similar to any other peer-to-peer system, Bitcoin incorporates a set of mechanisms aimed at identifying fresh nodes within the network and upholding an up-to-date roster thereof. Furthermore, particular Bitcoin clients, such as the Satoshi client, have the capacity to provide supplementary mechanisms. The add and retrieve add messages are particularly noteworthy among the primary alternatives. This feature enables a client to engage in communication (or make a query) regarding the list of currently connected clients on the network. Typically, the client code also incorporates a roster of seed nodes. In the event that alternative methods prove ineffective, this option may be employed to establish a connection with the network. "The seed nodes comprised within the December 2013 edition of the "official" Satoshi client were:

• The domain seed.bitcoin.sipa.be

• The website address is bitseed.xf2.org.

• Requirement. Blue matt.me

The domain dnsseed.bitcoin.dashjr.org can be utilized for this purpose.

In addition to methods employed for discovering alternative nodes within the network, a variety of communication mechanisms find extensive utilization in the realm of Bitcoin. The tx and block messages, for instance, serve the purpose of transmitting transaction data and blocks, correspondingly. The nodes within the network have the ability to uphold the synchronization prerequisites of the protocol. Additionally, they utilize inv type messages to broadcast the notification of novel transactions.

Bitcoin Data Structures

Wallets and Addresses

A Bitcoin address comprises the public and private keys derived from the ECDSA algorithm. The public key hash is employed to ascertain the address which is then multiplied by the checksum. Subsequently, this information is encoded using a modified variant of base 58, whereby the encoding process retains any leading zeros.

All actions performed using this address must be supported by the appropriate private key subsequent to being authenticated by the ECDSA public key. Wallets consist of a consolidation of both public and private keys. This does not constrain the usage of wallets to perform additional activities, such as facilitating transactions.

Transactions

Bitcoin transactions are recorded through digital signatures, thereby transferring ownership of Bitcoin funds by assigning them to a different address. A transaction comprises the ensuing elements, effectively defining the framework depicted in Figure 3:

• Inputs: documents that make reference to transactions that occurred in the past

- Results: documents that establish the updated proprietor of the transferred bitcoins.

Figure 5. Bitcoin Transaction

The resulting outputs are subsequently employed as new inputs in subsequent operations. In addition, it should be noted that all bitcoins in the output addresses are consistently utilized. This means that the total sum of outputs cannot be fragmented, even in cases where it exceeds the required payment amount. In the event that this is so, an alternative outcome is generated, whereby the purchaser would receive 'change'.

Figure 6. Transaction Fields

The initiator of the transaction provides digital verification for each transaction input, thereby authorizing the release of funds from the address associated with the corresponding private key used in the authentication process. Exclusively the principal proprietor of the corresponding private key possesses the capability to generate an authentic signature using this methodology. This guarantees that the funds can solely be utilized by the individual in possession of them. The aforementioned procedure is depicted in Figure 7.

Figure 7. Transaction Signatures

The outcomes comprise the address of
the payee and, if deemed necessary, an
address possessed by the payer for
receiving any potential change. In the
context of a transaction, it is imperative
for the total value of the inputs to be

either equal to or surpass that of the outputs. In the event that the input of bitcoins exceeds the output, the disparity is regarded as a transaction fee, which can be utilized by the entity incorporating this transaction into the blockchain. This acts as an incentive for miners, who receive bitcoins as a compensation for their efforts. Payers typically determine the fee incorporated within their payments (though numerous Bitcoin clients utilize default values). Hence, it is customary for transactions accompanied by higher fees (referred to as rewards) to undergo more expedited processing compared to those with lower fees.

Additionally, there exist exclusive transactions that arise from the process of generating new bitcoins via mining, wherein there are no preceding inputs involved. There exists a marginal yet significant differentiation between Bitcoin and genuine monetary systems in regards to the act of theft. When an individual appropriates tangible currency, the lawful proprietor consequently forfeits the ability to use it, as its physical presence transitions into the (illicit) ownership of the criminal. In the context of Bitcoin, should an individual "appropriate" the private keys associated with bitcoins, the act of theft would not be operationally viable until the perpetrator proceeds to transfer the pilfered bitcoins into an account under their control. Alternatively, in the event that the lawful owner possesses knowledge of the aforementioned private keys, they can proceed to transfer said keys to a new account, of which the thief remains oblivious to the corresponding private key. This course of action effectively impedes the successful execution of the theft.

A Bitcoin transaction can be outlined as the ensuing process:

- A compilation of Bitcoin addresses,

- Transferring a multitude of Bitcoins,

- An inventory of Bitcoin addresses • A catalog of Bitcoin addresses • A compilation of Bitcoin addresses • An enumeration of Bitcoin addresses • A roster of Bitcoin addresses

What happens in a transaction is that a user sends or receives a script. Through the validation of the script, one can initiate the process of withdrawing Bitcoins. Bitcoin transactions do not singularly encompass exchanges between two specific addresses. There exists no practical restriction on the quantity of individuals who can act as both senders and recipients in this context. This observation is intriguing due to the intriguing attributes it presents. For example, it may be necessary to establish a predetermined minimum value for a transaction to be transmitted.

That makes it possible for a third party to supervise a transaction, which can carry the role of the credit card company, which avoids fraud. The sole distinction lies in the fact that these services can be provided on a marketplace devoid of any counterparty risk. The transaction lacks any form of encryption, yet it is pseudonymous. Given that the senders and receivers are represented by public keys, their identities remain indiscernible to external observers. When initiating transactions on the network, it is possible to include an optional fee along with the transactions. This facilitates expedited transactions, which will be discussed in the subsequent section.

When initiating a transaction, it undergoes immediate dissemination throughout the entire network. The nodes have a rapid recognition of a transaction within a matter of seconds, although it requires additional time for the transaction to be fully confirmed. In the event that a hacker gains control over multiple nodes, it becomes possible to execute a double-spending attack targeted at a singular entity. Consequently, in the event of a more substantial transaction, it is imperative to await the receipt of multiple confirmations. The initial acknowledgment indicates that the transaction has been incorporated into a block, while subsequent confirmations indicate the addition of blocks to extend the blockchain. Once a transaction has been confirmed six times, it attains a level of security that inspires trust from all parties involved.

Instagram/Facebook Page

This technique is equally impressive in its ability to initiate the accumulation of affiliate commissions. The mechanism of operation is strikingly similar to that of YouTube. Prior to commencing promotional activities, it is imperative to cultivate a dedicated audience for your page. To provide a comprehensive explanation, it can be stated as follows: in the absence of an audience, the outcome will inevitably be a lack of sales. Hence, our paramount objective is to enhance the size of our Instagram page, thereby leading to increased affiliate commission.

One potential approach would involve establishing a Facebook page tailored to your particular field of interest. Now that you have established an Instagram account and a Facebook page, commence the promotion of both platforms by acquiring endorsements exclusively through the procurement of shoutouts from influential pages within your specific industry. Once that task is completed, you will gradually initiate the expansion of your Instagram/Facebook page. However, it is crucial to bear in mind that abstaining from posting content on your Instagram/Facebook page may lead to a decrease in followers and engagement.

The subsequent approach to expand your Instagram page involves the utilization of a method commonly referred to as the "follow-unfollow" technique. Its concept is fairly straightforward and easy to comprehend. An effective strategy entails initiating user engagements by following individuals in the hope of gaining reciprocal follows, and subsequently, discreetly unfollowing them at a later stage. This approach proves effective in rapidly acquiring a substantial following. Having said that, it is imperative to bear in mind that this approach may not be conducive to sustained long-term development. Commence the act of tracking individuals, subsequently terminating said tracking after approximately three days.

Lastly, we shall now delve into the strategies for generating income through affiliate marketing on Instagram. After amassing a following of approximately 100k, you will begin to observe individuals offering remuneration in exchange for featuring their products on your platform. In addition, it is possible to engage in affiliate marketing through ClickBank; however, the effectiveness is notably enhanced when employing the "shoutout" technique on Instagram for promotional purposes.

Employing the three simultaneously

Under the ideal circumstances, this is the expected outcome. Employing a combination of YouTube, Blogging, and Instagram concurrently will generate the most favorable outcomes. If your objective is to generate substantial financial gains through affiliate marketing, allow me to outline the necessary steps in achieving this goal. Your initial task will involve establishing a brand. As an illustration, in the event that you possess a keen interest in fitness, you would establish a YouTube channel, blog, and Instagram/Facebook profile under a self-conceived brand appellation. Now, you shall employ the techniques elucidated in this with the intention of fostering the growth and prosperity of all three sales channels, namely YouTube, blog, and Instagram.

What is the potential income that can be generated?

Presently, this inquiry eludes an immediate response. It should be noted that if your objective is to allocate the least amount of time and strive for maximum passivity, it is feasible to generate a monthly income ranging between $100 and $1,000. However, if you are genuinely inclined towards generating substantial profits and implement all three sales channels in conjunction with the aforementioned strategies, you have the potential to earn monthly revenues ranging from $100,000 to $1,000,000. Based on my firsthand observations, I have had the opportunity to review pay stubs belonging to the most successful affiliate marketers. Their annual earnings consistently surpass the million-dollar mark; thus, with a strong commitment to diligent effort, it is entirely attainable to generate a substantial income.

Having considered all aspects discussed, I would like to bring this to a close by stating the following: When it comes to affiliate marketing, the decision ultimately rests in your hands. You have the option to augment your monthly earnings by $1,000 through sporadic work, or alternatively, you can truly elevate your income. Once more, the decision rests in your hands.

3: The Ethereum Virtual Machine

The primary focus of the virtual machine will be on ensuring the security and proper execution of untrusted code implemented by globally utilized computers. If you desire a more thorough analysis, your attention will be directed towards the study of DOS attacks and their prevention. These attacks, also known as denial of service attacks, are increasingly prevalent within the realm of cryptocurrency. In addition, the virtual machine guarantees that the state of one program remains inaccessible to other programs, as it establishes interference-free communication channels.

While this may appear to be a concept that eludes your understanding, we shall articulate it in a manner that aligns with your comprehension.

The Ethereum virtual machine is poised to function as a runtime environment for the smart contracts present within Ethereum. A significant number of cryptocurrency users possess full knowledge of the concept of smart contracts and are keenly aware of their widespread popularity. This technology possesses the capability to execute transactions autonomously or undertake actions on the blockchain without necessitating supervision. It is widely held that smart contracts possess the potential to profoundly transform the financial sector in the foreseeable future.

Furthermore, it is of note that the concept of the virtual machine can be traced back to a scholarly publication authored by Dr. Gavin Wood, emphasizing the proposition that Ethereum was developed with the intent to usher in a controlled and isolated computational environment that carries transformative implications for the foreseeable future. The utilization of smart contracts serves as a pivotal element of code that contributes to enhancing Ethereum's superiority over alternative platforms.

When considering sandboxed environments, one cannot underestimate the potential they hold for technology, despite being in its nascent stage and undergoing constant evolution.

Once the decentralization of day-to-day operations is implemented, it will become apparent how the virtual machine operates to effectively carry out this undertaking.

Furthermore, the virtual machine possesses significant value and is readily accessible without any cost. Wouldn't software developers welcome such an opportunity?

Understanding The Principles Behind Blockchain Technology

What is blockchain?

In essence, the blockchain technology can be described as a distributed ledger system that operates in a decentralized and public manner. It maintains a registry of transactions while ensuring a stringent level of security.

The blockchain, formerly known as block chain (in separate words), comprises a collection of records known as blocks. The interconnection of these blocks relies on cryptographic measures for enhanced security. Cryptography entails the safeguarding of communication. It pertains to the confidentiality and safeguarding of information.

Each block within the chain is connected to a preceding block through the utilization of a hash pointer. Additionally, a time stamp and transaction information are also included. The integrity of each block or record is safeguarded by the blockchain, which diligently documents transactions across a distributed network of computers. By employing this method, it is impossible to alter or modify any record without simultaneously modifying the entire sequence of blocks. As a publicly accessible ledger, all users have the ability to scrutinize and examine each and every transaction. Due to its decentralized nature, the blockchain technology operates autonomously without being subjected to the control or influence of any central governing body. The alteration of records within a blockchain by its founder or developer requires the unanimous consent or prior notification of all other participants.

A concise overview of the origins and development of blockchain technology

When discussing the historical origins of blockchain technology, it is generally perceived that its initial development can be attributed to Satoshi Nakamoto. Nevertheless, it is pertinent to acknowledge that the initial effort to establish a secure sequence of interconnected blocks using cryptographic methods was undertaken in 1991 by the individual identified as W. Scott Stornetta and Stuart Haber, researchers who have made notable contributions in this field. Nevertheless, the task was deemed unfinished and devoid of certain essential components. The situation changed in 2008 with the arrival and conceptualization by Satoshi Nakamoto of a blockchain technology that fueled the creation of Bitcoin, a cryptocurrency that emerged the subsequent year. The initial distributed blockchain in existence was developed by Satoshi Nakamoto. Therefore, it is widely considered that Satoshi Nakamoto is the individual responsible for the development and establishment of blockchain technology.

How does blockchain work?

Please find below an elucidation of the procedures involved in a transaction on a blockchain: X intends to transfer a certain amount of funds to Z. This transaction shall be denoted as a block. Subsequently, this block will be disseminated to all the entities within the network. All members within the network shall confirm the aforementioned transaction as legitimate. Upon verification, the aforementioned block will be appended to the chain, thereby facilitating the transfer of funds from X to Z.

Structure of the blockchain: the shaded blocks indicate the primary chain. Orphan blocks reside outside the primary chain.

It is noteworthy that the blockchain technology is undergoing a revolutionary transformation, not solely due to its application in facilitating cryptocurrency transactions, but rather due to its potential to encompass all types of value-based transactions. As a result, it encompasses not only cryptocurrency or money, but also extends to encompassing goods and property.

Gaining insights into the blockchain database.

When observing a blockchain database, one would encounter two key components: blocks and transactions. What is a block? A block refers to a legitimate transaction that has been hashed and encoded within the blockchain. To establish linkage with the preceding block, each subsequent block incorporates the hash value of its antecedent block.

Here is an illustrative instance: Consider the scenario where individual A engages in the transfer of bitcoins to individual B. The blockchain will display person A's wallet address alongside the associated cryptocurrency value being transferred to B. Indeed, the identities of both A and B will remain anonymous throughout the network, with only their respective wallet addresses and the corresponding transaction amounts being displayed. The blockchain shall exhibit and maintain a comprehensive log of the transaction, encompassing an accurately recorded timestamp. In addition, it will demonstrate the transactions that have already been verified, alongside those that are still pending confirmation.

When making reference to a sequence of connected blocks, the term commonly employed is 'chain'. Evidently, comprehending the blockchain technology does not pose significant difficulty. The ongoing linkage of each block to its predecessor persists until reaching the genesis block. The inaugural block establishes the initial foundation of a blockchain.

Could you please explain the concept of a distributed ledger?

Could you kindly provide an elaboration on the functionalities and purpose of a distributed ledger? The notion of a distributed ledger entails that any alterations made to the ledger shall be disseminated to and harmonized across the entirety of the network. As an illustration, if X were to make a modification to the ledger, the aforementioned modification would be automatically reflected on Y's ledger, provided that they are part of the same blockchain. The aforementioned alteration will be visible to other participants on the blockchain. Please be advised that the users within a blockchain system do not have access to distinct ledgers of one another. Instead, the entire network of the blockchain operates on a singular ledger, facilitating immediate and simultaneous dissemination of all modifications throughout the network.

The underlying principle of the 51% attack.

The term '51% attack' pertains to the integrity of the blockchain technology. This implies that in order for a blockchain attack to achieve success, it is required for the attacker to possess a minimum of 51% of the entire hash rate of the targeted blockchain network. Please be informed that the blockchain network is comprised of an extensive array of computers, resulting in a significantly elevated hash rate. This renders it virtually impregnable against any assault.

It is important to acknowledge that the notion of a 51% concept does not imply that a blockchain is immune to attacks. It remains conceivable to launch an assault on a blockchain even when the hash rate is below the threshold of 51%. Nevertheless, it is unlikely that such an assault would yield any measure of success. Furthermore, it should be noted that a malicious attempt employing a hash rate exceeding 51% does not necessarily ensure the accomplishment of the aforementioned attack.

Smart contract

A smart contract entails a programmable code that exists within a distributed network of interconnected blocks. It establishes the parameters, and upon fulfillment of these parameters, the contract shall be executed by all computers within the network. This provides users with the reassurance of achieving the intended result. Smart contracts have the potential to be utilized within the context of blockchain technology. Currently, the cryptocurrency widely recognized for its utilization of smart contracts is Ethereum. Ethereum is widely regarded as one of the foremost cryptocurrencies that has achieved remarkable success within the current market landscape. Currently, it holds the second highest position in terms of rank, trailing only after bitcoin.

Here is an illustrative instance that elucidates the functionality of smart contracts: Let us consider a scenario where the shipper, identified as W, is entrusted with the responsibility of delivering a specific item to an individual named Z. While Z places trust in W, the individual entrusted with the responsibility of delivering the item, he harbors a lack of trust in X. Therefore, Z will engage in a contractual arrangement with W to solely make payment for the item upon its delivery. This is being done in order to ensure adherence, particularly in this scenario where Z harbors doubts regarding the individual responsible for delivering the item. Nevertheless, this methodology is rather intricate and typically entails the involvement of external entities. Additionally, there is the possibility of a predicament arising in the event that W wishes to ensure receipt of payment but disagrees with the terms put forth by Z.

With the implementation of smart contracts, this process can be streamlined. Rather than transmitting the payment to W, Z only needs to remit the shipment payment to a smart contract at the time of loading. The intelligent agreement will subsequently retain the aforementioned payment until Z validates the receipt of the merchandise. Once the delivery is complete and confirmed, the funds paid by Z will be promptly disbursed to W.

Smart contracts not only establish the conditions, but also possess the capability to execute the provisions of the contracts. This renders them exceedingly adaptable. Although it is indeed true that, presently, smart contracts can solely process basic terms or tasks, one can envision the vast expansion of their capabilities in dealing with intricate terms and executing tasks by deploying a significant number of smart contracts.

5: The Procurement and Trade of Bitcoin and Ethereum

Bitcoin

Buying

Firstly, it is possible to acquire Bitcoins through exchanges or by engaging in direct transactions with individuals within the marketplace. There exist various forms of payment available, including cash, debit or credit cards, wire transfers, or the utilization of alternative cryptocurrencies, contingent upon the vendor and the purchaser's jurisdiction of residence. Acquiring Bitcoins using a credit card or PayPal presents considerable challenges. This is primarily due to the fact that the transactions can be reversed by contacting the respective companies. The range of possibilities for conducting financial transfers has expanded in certain nations. In the United States, clients have the option to utilize the services of express coin, which has recently begun accepting alternative forms of payment such as money orders, wire transfers, and personal checks.

One can acquire a variety of wallets based on the preferred level of security. Several wallets cater to daily expenses, while alternative wallets adhere to more stringent operational protocols. The three primary alternatives consist of a software wallet that is stored on the hard drive of your computer, a web-based service, and an online vault wallet that securely stores your Bitcoins offline.

Numerous companies provide services for exchanges and online wallets. Certain establishments are renowned enterprises, while others consist of ordinary merchants endeavoring to establish themselves. The exchanges will provide a storage solution for your digital currency. If your intention is to participate in substantial trading activities, it is advisable to utilize exchanges and wallets as the most suitable choice. They assist in circumventing any bureaucratic formalities and maintaining confidentiality associated with the establishment of an account. A selection of exchange companies that can be considered comprises the following: Coinbase (located in the United States of America), LocalBitcoins (based in Finland), Bit Quick (operating out of the

United States of America), BitBargain (headquartered in the United Kingdom), Xapo (situated in the United States of America), and Unocoin (operating in India).

The majority of companies require evidence of identity, whereby wallets and exchanges fail to provide equivalent safeguards as financial institutions. Frequently, the possibility of inadequate or restricted account insurance exists in the event of unauthorized access or hacking. Bitcoins lack legal recognition as a legitimate currency in the majority of jurisdictions worldwide. Consequently, judicial entities lack a definitive strategy for addressing these theft incidents. Furthermore, in the event of a wallet theft resulting from a negligence on your part with respect to the PIN number, there is no recourse available for recovering your funds. Certain financial institutions exhibit bias towards transactions involving digital currency.

The majority of Bitcoin wallets provide a Bitcoin private key, which is required for both storage and expenditure of your Bitcoins. In a manner similar to safeguarding physical wallets, users ensure the security of their Bitcoins. The private key governs the transactions associated with your account.

The most convenient method of obtaining Bitcoins is via direct in-person transactions. Gather in populated public areas. LocalBitcoins serves as the foremost platform for conducting this particular transaction. The website facilitates an escrow service, thereby affording an additional layer of protection for all involved parties. ATM services are provided by vendors such as Bit Access, Coin Outlet, and Genesis Coin. Prior to receiving a paper receipt, it is necessary to both insert your cash and scan the provided QR code. The currency exchange rates exhibit an increment of up to 8% compared to the standard rates.

In summary, numerous establishments offer the opportunity to purchase Bitcoins. Prioritize the implementation of robust security measures to safeguard transactions, as any loss of digital currency cannot be reimbursed.

Selling

The purchasing and vending procedures for Bitcoins exhibit variances, with the latter being potentially less straightforward than the former. Rest assured, there are multiple avenues through which you can liquidate your Bitcoin holdings. One must take into consideration the most suitable approach for oneself. This entails two primary alternatives, wherein you have the option to either convert your currency into cash through online means or via an in-person transaction. It is evident that every alternative possesses its corresponding advantages and disadvantages which it is imperative for you to comprehend in advance.

Examining each of them will facilitate the process of determining the optimal choice to pursue in your transaction.

Selling Online

This is the predominant method of selling Bitcoins, comprising three primary modalities.

Employing direct exchanges

This can be accomplished via various online platforms that provide this particular service. Among the platforms that fall into this category is Coinbase, which is based in the United States, alongside LocalBitcoins. BitBargain and Bittylicious are both reputable options for facilitating cryptocurrency transactions within the United Kingdom. Within this platform, you have the opportunity to formally register as a seller and create a listing for your merchandise. Rest assured, you will receive timely notifications regarding the availability of prospective buyers interested in engaging in trade with you.

This will enable you to establish communication with them and successfully carry out the transaction through the online platform.

Exchange trades

This alternative necessitates the process of enrolling with an internet-based exchange platform and undergoing identity authentication. Nonetheless, the most advantageous aspect of exchange trades is the minimal level of engagement required in executing the transaction. In this instance, you simply initiate a purchase request, akin to the process employed for a buy order. Please ensure that you provide detailed information on the currency type, quantity, and individual unit price. In the event that an individual presents a valid purchase order, the transaction shall be automatically executed, thereby resulting in the transfer of the corresponding currency to your designated account.

Nevertheless, if you intend to exchange Bitcoins for traditional currencies, you may encounter challenges related to liquidity and banking institutions. Consequently, this could lead to prolonged waiting periods before receiving the desired funds.

Decentralized trading platforms

Websites such as Purse and Brawker are notable for providing these services with ease and convenience. These websites facilitate the convergence of individuals with similar requirements. Groups consist of individuals who desire to utilize Bitcoins for transactions on platforms that do not facilitate digital currencies, as well as those endeavoring to acquire Bitcoins through credit or debit card transactions. Consequently, these individuals have the ability to engage in the exchange of Bitcoins and acquire discounted merchandise from one another.

An inherent drawback associated with online transactions lies in the requirement of identity verification, which tends to be less stringent for buyers but more demanding for sellers. Another point of concern pertains to the matter of fund withdrawals, which could potentially be intricate and time-consuming in certain instances.

Selling Offline

This alternative provides a slightly more convenient option, whereby it is possible to facilitate the transaction by utilizing a QR code scanner on a third party's device to receive the funds. Additionally, it is possible to transfer Bitcoins to a friend or family member and promptly receive the corresponding funds. This calls for the examination of matters such as the establishment of pricing consensus and ensuring safety measures. Prioritizing safety is of utmost importance, particularly in cases where a substantial sum of money is at stake. You have the option of convening in a public setting or inviting a companion to accompany you.

Monitoring Software

As Bitcoins and the encompassing markets operate continuously, it is imperative for traders to seek software that facilitates constant market monitoring. Automated trading systems facilitate continuous real-time transaction monitoring for traders. Automated trading software, known as Trading Bots, is integrated with exchanges to implement strategies when traders are away from their computers or occupied with other tasks. Trading bots are a form of automated systems designed to generate financial gains.

Haasbot and Tradewave are software solutions that can be readily accessed in the marketplace. Cryptotrader can be characterized as a type of cloud-hosted software. Every individual software elicited different responses from the exchanges, thereby resulting in the placement of buy or sell bids accordingly. The offers generated by the software can be inputted manually. Nevertheless, they serve as a substitute for the absence of the dealer. By means of pre-programming, various types of software have the capacity to initiate one or more transactions in the market autonomously, thereby eliminating the need for continuous monitoring of the trading system.

The founder of Haasbot outlines a purchasing strategy whereby individuals can acquire a certain quantity of Bitcoins in advance and implement a predetermined selling approach for capitalizing on significant market price increases. Hence, the dealer will not incur any form of financial detriment.

De Hass, the director of Haasbot, contends that by leveraging technical analysis expertise, the utilization of trading bots confers a competitive edge for traders, distinguishing them from those who do not employ any trading strategies.

Trading Bots provide a safeguard by restricting the trading of Bitcoins once the trading rates have depreciated. In the event of a market downturn during the trader's absence, the resultant impact on their business would be minimal.

Certain traders display doubt regarding the effectiveness of automated systems, emphasizing the necessity for traders to actively engage in decision-making. Without explicit programming for purchasing or selling a specific quantity of shares, software remains incapable of autonomous operation. The rationale behind not programming trading bots to carry out specific functions is the focal point of the argument put forth. In accordance with the analysis of the traders, it is expected that trading bots should not simply be viewed as a tool, but rather as a comprehensive solution.

However, the effectiveness of trading Bots remains contingent upon the actions and decisions made by the end user. Having proficiency in technical analysis can prove advantageous in the initial stages of programming trading bots. It assists traders in mitigating losses.

Trading algorithms can assist traders in capitalizing on market inefficiencies, particularly through activities such as market making and executing arbitrary trades. For instance, in situations where there is a discrepancy in Bitcoin prices between different market channels, algorithmic trading bots are capable of facilitating multiple exchanges. Attainment of arbitrary trading can be realized by submitting inflated bids on exchanges with limited trading activity.

Automated trading systems can exploit market inefficiencies, particularly in the context of electronic execution of substantial orders. The Flashcard bot has the capacity to engage in a range of five to fifteen transactions throughout the day, particularly when the price fluctuations of trading bots are significant. Nonetheless, the utilization of trading inefficiencies by numerous marketers will ultimately lead to the absence of any inefficiencies. The Eliosoff trading fund advocates for the utilization of Algorithmic market strategy, whereby trading orders are executed for substantial volumes on a singular exchange.

There is no guaranteed method of achieving profitable trading results through automated bots. Whenever a software tool is introduced to the market, it eventually loses its efficiency due to the widespread adoption by numerous users. The efficacy of the trading bots relies upon the aptitude of individual traders in effectively pre-programming them.

Guidance For Novices

Having been made cognizant of the primary merits and demerits associated with cryptocurrency, it is likely that you now possess a more discerning understanding of the advantages and risks entailed in its utilization.

By now, you may have developed either a heightened reluctance towards embracing the cryptocurrency trend or an increased level of interest in it. If you belong to the latter category, it would be more advantageous for you to acquaint yourself with a set of constructive recommendations for individuals who are new to the world of cryptocurrency.

The greater amount of information you possess, the higher likelihood you would have of making astute decisions in order to maximize the effectiveness of your financial resources. Unless you possess an inherent desire for excitement or a penchant for gambling, it is likely that you would derive substantial benefit from a comprehensive set of guidance that could prove invaluable in the foreseeable future.

Invalidate sources of information that exhibit bias.

When conducting research, it is recommended to seek out sources that have a strong reputation and refrain from excessive advertising or bias towards promoting singular cryptocurrency investments. Please be advised that there is a substantial presence of fraudulent individuals who create websites with the sole intention of luring inexperienced individuals through deceptive information and aggressive marketing tactics. Sources that exhibit a greater degree of objectivity and impartiality can be deemed more reliable, as they encompass comprehensive information on a specific product, such as a particular cryptocurrency, by including both positive and negative aspects.

Allocate capital judiciously and in accordance with your financial resources.

As previously mentioned, it is strongly advised against allocating all of one's resources into cryptocurrency investments. This applies to all forms of investment. Commencing with modest beginnings and harboring optimism is consistently a more prudent approach. In the event that you generate income, it is indeed commendable. Conversely, should you encounter any financial losses, it should not precipitate a state of insurmountable debt or lead to a complete depletion of your financial resources.

Developing Feasible Objectives within Your Reach

Please bear in mind that cryptocurrency does not offer a means to swiftly accumulate wealth. Adopt a practical approach when establishing your investment goals regarding the potential returns of cryptocurrency. Additionally, it is important to bear in mind that the cryptocurrency market is highly volatile, necessitating your commitment to remain invested even during periods of decline.

Exert self-control in refraining from succumbing to panic

Conduct thorough research and familiarize yourself with the cryptocurrency market prior to commencing your endeavors. Engaging in this practice can diminish your proclivity to experience panic and exhibit impulsive behavior in subsequent situations.

Strive to Exercise Sound Judgment

When engaging with cryptocurrency, or any other form of investment, one should refrain from making speculative assumptions about future market movements. The investment markets frequently exhibit volatility, necessitating careful consideration and prudent decision-making when evaluating cryptocurrency options. In order to make informed decisions, it is imperative that one engages in diligent research and exertion of effort. By closely monitoring the cryptocurrency market, one can effectively discern its prevailing trends.

Acquire knowledge from your mistakes

It cannot be overstated - the cryptocurrency market exhibits significant volatility, and it is plausible that an unfavorable decision regarding your cryptocurrency holdings may arise. In such a circumstance, it is crucial to maintain persistence and refrain from surrendering. Alternatively, endeavor to ascertain the factors that led to the mishap and determine the root cause behind your mistake. Gain knowledge from your mistakes in order to progress.

Devise Your Strategic Plan

Acquire the capability to discern and adhere to the fluctuations within the cryptocurrency market, thereby enhancing your comprehension of it. It would be advantageous to acquire the knowledge of chart analysis and ensure diligent real-time monitoring of your investments. By engaging in this process, you will have the opportunity to devise strategies for executing the subsequent stages of your cryptocurrency investment.

Do not be left behind" "Ensure you do not get left behind" "Take measures to avoid being left behind" "Make sure not to fall behind" "Stay ahead to avoid being left behind

To maximize the benefits of your cryptocurrency investment, it is imperative to acquire knowledge and understanding. As your knowledge expands, so too will your understanding and discernment in navigating the realm of cryptocurrency, enabling you to make informed decisions when engaging in buying, selling, utilizing, or exchanging digital assets. As proverbial wisdom suggests, the acquisition of knowledge empowers individuals, thus it is highly encouraged to diligently seek and amass knowledge to the fullest extent possible.

These are straightforward yet valuable recommendations, and it is at your discretion to adhere to them or devise your own strategies for achieving success in the realm of cryptocurrency.

Cryptocurrency Security

The security of cryptocurrencies can be viewed as consisting of two components. The first component originates from the challenge of locating intersections within hash sets, which is a task undertaken by miners. The second and more probable scenario is a "51% attack." In this particular situation, should a miner possess a mining capacity exceeding 51% of the network, they would be capable of assuming control over the overarching blockchain ledger and subsequently producing an alternative blockchain. At present juncture, the assailant's capabilities remain restricted. The assailant possesses the capability to undo his own transactions or obstruct the progress of other transactions.

Cryptocurrencies are also less vulnerable to being seized by law enforcement entities or encountering transaction holds imposed by acquirers like Paypal. All digital currencies possess a pseudo-anonymous nature, while certain coins incorporate supplementary functionalities to achieve genuine anonymity.

Legality Of Cryptocurrencies

With the increasing integration of cryptocurrencies into society, global law enforcement agencies, tax authorities, and legal regulators are endeavoring to comprehend the fundamental notion of digital currencies and their precise position within current regulatory and legal structures.

The advent of Bitcoin ushered in an entirely novel paradigm, establishing it as the pioneering cryptocurrency. As anticipated, the advent of decentralized and self-sufficient virtual currencies, devoid of tangible representation and independent of singular governance, was destined to elicit unrest within regulatory circles.

Numerous apprehensions have been voiced pertaining to the decentralized nature of cryptocurrencies and their propensity to be utilized with a high degree of anonymity. Global authorities have expressed concerns regarding the allure of cryptocurrencies among traders involved in illicit transactions. Additionally, they express concerns regarding their potential involvement in illicit activities such as money laundering and tax evasion.

As of November 2017, the use and trade of Bitcoin and other digital currencies are prohibited exclusively in Bangladesh, Bolivia, Ecuador, Kyrgyzstan, and Vietnam, with China and Russia edging towards the implementation of bans on these currencies. In contrast, other governmental bodies have not yet enacted prohibitions on the utilization of cryptocurrencies, although it should be noted that legislation and regulatory frameworks may significantly differ from one nation to another.

Although cryptocurrencies are considered legal in the majority of countries, there are a few exceptions such as Iceland and Vietnam. Iceland, specifically, has implemented regulations and restrictions on cryptocurrency due to their strict control over foreign exchange. China has implemented a prohibition on bitcoin transactions by financial institutions, while Russia, despite recognizing cryptocurrency as lawful, has criminalized the use of any currency other than the Russian ruble for purchasing commodities.

In accordance with the decision of the Internal Revenue Service (IRS) in the United States, Bitcoin is classified as property for taxation purposes, and is thus liable to capital gains tax. Guidelines for cryptocurrencies have been issued by the Financial Crimes Enforcement Network (FinCEN). The guidelines provided include a significant caveat for individuals engaged in Bitcoin mining: it cautions that those involved in the creation of bitcoins and subsequent conversion to fiat currency may still be subject to legal consequences. It states:

An individual who generates convertible virtual currency units and subsequently exchanges them with another individual for real currency or its equivalent is involved in the act of transferring to a different destination and is classified as a money transmitter."

It appears that miners can be classified under this category, thereby potentially rendering them accountable for MTB classification. This matter has become a subject of disagreement among bitcoin miners, who have requested further elucidation. To this day, there has been no public legal resolution of this matter in a court of law.

Blockchain: Opinion Or Science?

A significant portion of the populace lacks comprehension of this technology due to its potential to fundamentally alter the functioning of our economy in the foreseeable future. What if we were empowered to autonomously manage the economy, engaging in transactions and determining price levels independently, unfettered by the involvement of governmental entities or financial institutions, thus eliminating concerns regarding monetary and temporal inefficiencies? Blockchain has the capability to facilitate this outcome.

Financial institutions continue to exist in the contemporary technological landscape, albeit viewed as antiquated concepts. Certain processes within their operations have experienced an expedited pace facilitated by the utilization of the Internet. Currently, the majority of account holders are able to conduct their financial transactions without the need for direct communication with personnel at the respective financial institutions. The funds present within these financial institutions are transitioning towards a virtual form, as an increasing number of individuals rely on credit and debit cards instead of physical currency.

Despite the occurrence of these events and the increasingly digitized nature of money and online communication, the majority of financial systems have yet to make significant advancements. They continue to remain connected to verification systems and securities transfers that are unable to meet the demands of the integrated contemporary world.

This is the reason why the concept of blockchains can be highly invigorating and is poised to fundamentally transform the conduct of the financial sector in the forthcoming years. These developments will have a transformative impact on the way governments, financial institutions, and individuals engage with monetary transactions in the years to come.

What is the Impact of This on the Economy?

Although various establishments are endeavoring to innovate their financial records, the fundamental concept remains consistent with certain conventional practices they have employed in the past. The compilation process of these ledgers is time-consuming and, regrettably, their level of security and accuracy does not always meet the standards expected by these financial institutions. Indeed, these instances frequently result in financial implications amounting to millions of dollars for the financial institution annually.

However, by leveraging blockchain technology, a portion of these difficulties can be effectively addressed. As per Santander's analysis, it has projected that the implementation of blockchain technology has the potential to enable the United States to achieve cost savings of up to $20 billion by the year 2022. Furthermore, this technology holds promise for other nations, as it offers the opportunity to enhance operational efficiency and effectiveness, leading to similar or even greater financial savings. Numerous private financial institutions are already exhibiting enthusiasm towards this variety of technology, and are undertaking initiatives to implement blockchain technology in order to document their respective transactions.

Blockchains exhibit stark differences from the antiquated financial systems that prevail. It was the product of extensive refinement spanning several decades, a crucial aspect given the contemporary vulnerability of the antiquated system, previously regarded as impervious, due to the increasing prevalence of hacking activities. Fortunately, the design of the blockchain ensures the concealment of code fragments within a hash. Consequently, any attempts to tamper with the records become immediately apparent, as the altered hash values left by the hacker will inevitably deviate from their expected counterparts.

Therefore, blockchain technology is characterized by enhanced usability and efficiency relative to alternative methods employed in the domains of e-commerce and banking, while simultaneously affording superior levels of security. Blockchain has the ability to introduce a comprehensive level of transparency that is challenging to achieve with alternative methods, yet it holds significant importance in our contemporary digital society.

Now, let us consider a scenario where you intend to engage in a transaction with an individual residing in a foreign country. With the existing framework in place, it would be imperative for you to engage in collaboration with multiple counterparts, such as a virtual payment platform or an alternative financial institution, in order to achieve this objective. This could potentially incur significant costs and result in a considerable delay in the completion of the transaction. However, in a society wherein blockchain technology is integrated into the economic infrastructure, there would be no necessity for the presence of financial institutions, as the algorithms inherent in blockchain would suffice to authenticate all transactions, including those conducted across international borders. If there is a collective trust in this system and its functioning, the system will essentially serve as a self-regulator.

From the evidence presented, it becomes evident that blockchain technology possesses the potential to exert a profound impact on the forthcoming economy. It expedites transaction completion, facilitates trading with individuals residing in distant countries, and offers a level of security not currently attainable by other enterprises and online retailers.

Currently, the technology requires further refinement. Bitcoin currently stands as one of the foremost adopters of this technology, albeit confronted with challenges pertaining to illicit access by hackers and criminals who exploit the system and its ledger for personal gain. Due to the favorable reputation of the system underpinned by cryptocurrency, it follows that there exists a range of encryption mechanisms enabling substantial transparency and dependability in facilitating transactions among all involved parties. This demonstrates that, should a similar degree of trust be manifested within the financial sector, it has the potential to readily evolve into the desired future state of our economy.

4: Developing a Cryptocurrency Trading Strategy and Constructing a Well-Balanced Investment Portfolio

Given the surge in investor participation within the cryptocurrency sector, it becomes imperative to acquire comprehensive knowledge and resources pertaining to this subject matter. Possessing the ability to strategize trade preparations and maintain a well-balanced cryptocurrency portfolio provides traders with a distinct advantage in navigating the market. This will elucidate the rationale behind the importance of maintaining a well-structured cryptocurrency portfolio, adhering to a comprehensive trading strategy, and exercising the requisite discipline to meticulously execute said plan.

Crypto Trading Plan

A trading plan is a comprehensive strategic blueprint encompassing a determined set of guidelines that precisely articulate trading objectives and delineate assorted approaches to attain the predetermined objectives. It aids in maintaining concentration towards the implementation of strategies. In the realm of cryptocurrency, one can distinguish between two overarching categories of traders, namely discretionary traders and system traders. The discretionary traders are individuals who meticulously observe the market conditions and manually execute trades based on the available information, whereas the system traders employ a certain degree of trade automation to implement predefined rules.

Stock Markets

When contemplating engaging in cryptocurrency trading, it is prudent to carefully deliberate upon the stock markets on which one intends to execute said trades. Included within the sphere of trading markets are bonds, commodities, Exchange Traded Funds (ETFs), the Foreign Exchange (Forex), futures, options, as well as the widely renowned e-mini futures contracts. In order to optimize potential profit, it is imperative to select an instrument of sufficient liquidity and validity.

Liquidity refers to the level of ease in buying and selling shares. Markets characterized by narrow bid-ask spreads and substantial market depth, enabling prompt order execution, demonstrate favorable liquidity. It guarantees that orders will be processed with negligible spillage and without causing any impact on the prices.

However, it is worth noting that validity is a metric that assesses the rate of price fluctuations within a specific market. When a trading commodity experiences volatility, traders are presented with the chance to capitalize on price changes, regardless of whether these fluctuations result in an increase or decrease.

Optimal Timeframe for Decision-Making in Trading

Chart intervals are linked to a trading methodology that considers volume or market activity. Traders with long-term investment horizons exhibit a preference for employing charts encompassing lengthier time spans in their trading endeavors, whereas short-term traders opt for the utilization of charts that capture shorter time intervals. A brief time frame on a chart may extend to an hour, whereas a long-range chart can encompass a duration exceeding that. For instance, a scalper may demonstrate a preference for employing a 144-tick chart, whereas a swing trader tends to rely on the 60-minute chart.

A meticulously crafted trading plan should exhibit indicators that are relevant to the chart, notwithstanding the fact that indicators by themselves yield signals for purchase and sale. A trader ought to analyze the signals in order to identify entry and exit points that align with their distinctive trading approach.

Position Sizing

The position size can be defined as the monetary worth of a cryptocurrency that an individual is engaged in trading. The consideration of the trader's account size and risk tolerance is pivotal in determining the suitable sizing. Position sizing refers to the determination of the specific size of a position within a given investment portfolio. A prospective trader may opt to commence their activity by acquiring a single future contract. Once the system attains success, the trader may choose to allocate their investments towards alternative contracts. Engaging in the trading of multiple contracts enhances the potential for substantial profit margins by mitigating the risk of losses. Irrespective of the magnitude of investors' positions, all regulations are outlined in the trading plan.

Initiation of Trade Using Filters and Triggers

Individuals exhibit variations in their approach to engaging in trade. Maintaining a consistent approach when making an entry entails implementing pre-established trading regulations. Certain traders may exhibit a patient approach, closely observing the market from a position of inactivity while awaiting opportune moments to enter and allocate capital. This frequently places them in a position where they are on the brink of missing significant trading opportunities. They possess a conservative trading approach, in contrast to the aggressive traders who seize any available investment opportunity. Trade regulations cater to the needs and interests of both these entities, enabling them to derive advantages through the implementation of trade-based triggers and filters. Trade filters encompass diverse considerations, spanning from temporal aspects such as time of day to geographical aspects as the location of price. For instance, when employing a moving average, the closure of a price bar within a specific timeframe can prompt the initiation of another entry through the placement of a stop order above the preceding bar.

Exit Rules

Investing in cryptocurrency, regardless of the amount, can result in financial gains if you choose to sell at the optimal moment. The significance of exit points lies in their ability to determine the accomplishment of the trade. Some trade outcomes to consider upon exiting are as follows: levels of profit, employing stop and reverse strategies, and selecting specific time exits, such as at the end of the trading day.

The Challenges Posed by Regression to the Mean

It is imperative to have an understanding of the fact that the trading range has the ability to both contract and expand. The variability of price fluctuations on a daily basis has the potential to vary. Given that the average serves as the focal point, how can one ascertain the prevailing price range during periods of expansion and contraction within the range? It gets tricky then.

An additional aspect to consider when analyzing trading ranges is determining the appropriate historical extent necessary to deem a particular range significant. What would be the appropriate retrospective period for determining the range? For example, if we consider the 4-hour chart, it is possible to observe the price of the asset fluctuating within the limits of 1.4 and 1.9. Moreover, this can be perceived as a narrower range when compared to another range depicted on the daily chart, where the price varies between 0.5 and 4. The average you have chosen may encompass alternative averages based on a distinct time period. Please bear in mind that the markets display a fractal nature.

Additionally, one must contemplate the following inquiry: Are the prices of the security truly conforming to a normal distribution? Certain statisticians maintain that it is not so. According to anecdotal accounts, it has been suggested that the securities exhibit a semblance of normal distribution on certain occasions, yet in reality, this is not the case. As a technical analyst, it is incumbent upon you to ascertain the existence of a prevailing trend, its degree of strength, and the proximity at which it may potentially culminate. It is important to refrain from making assumptions about normal distribution, as doing so would essentially imply a precise understanding of where the trend will precisely reverse. Please be cognizant that in instances where the price exceeds one standard deviation, specifically when it surpasses a previous low or high, engaging in a mean-reversion strategy may result in your selling at a time when the price is poised to ascend. It is essential to bear in mind that mean-reversion trading entails a higher level of risk as compared to trend following due to the increased probability of making incorrect predictions.

Breakout Trading

In a scenario where there exists a domain of supply and demand, it is imperative to exercise caution during instances when significant news releases are anticipated. One can effectively monitor these releases by referencing complimentary online news calendars which will provide updates on when a particular event will impact your trading asset. It is advisable to refrain from engaging in news trading, as there is a risk of experiencing unfavorable price execution (slippage) or substantial losses resulting from sudden and significant market fluctuations in the opposite direction. Additionally, there is no assurance that your broker will execute your stop-loss order at the precise price that you have specified. This constitutes a formal contractual arrangement between you and your broker. It should be acknowledged that certain news occurrences hold a unique nature, such as the unprecedented tragic events that transpired on 9/11 or the unorthodox communication conducted by a global leader through social media platforms.

The perturbation resulting from this news precipitates a rupture, and it is challenging to ascertain whether the rupture will persist in alignment with its initial trajectory or if it is spurious. Primarily, breakouts indicate a shift in market sentiment towards security due to certain influencing factors. These individuals are frequently held in high regard, yet in cases where such admiration is lacking, they are colloquially referred to as "fake-outs" due to their transient nature and failure to initiate a novel trend. The price resumes its course to return to its previous range, which has been extended to a higher level.

Even the most inert trend will occasionally result in a substantial surge as a consequence of rumors and news. In the eventuality of such an occurrence, it becomes perplexing to comprehend the rationale behind considering the financial circumstances of each individual amongst the gathering. This is positioning. It impels price fluctuations devoid of discernible patterns or apparent logic, though indeed there exists an underlying cause for this phenomenon. Typically, the aforementioned information is held in confidence, restricted solely to individuals referred to as the "sharks." They possess constrained orders at particular market positions and possess the financial resources to induce tangible market fluctuations. For example, consider someone who is capable of making a sole investment of $5,000,000 in a specific sector of the economy. Remarkably, they have successfully augmented their account balance to $6,000,000 as a consequence. He will need to divest one million units in order to realize his gains. Position squaring entails the action of closing out positions within the market. This does not imply that the participants hold the belief that the prevailing trend has concluded. It is possible that they intend to revisit the trend in the future, possibly at a different time and price.

Position squaring occurs when individuals perceive that the trade has reached a temporary conclusion, achieved their desired profit or loss target, fulfilled their designated trading period or tax duration, or intend to accrue profits in order to seek an alternative security for trading. A similar occurrence arises when numerous traders sustain substantial losses. The traders concluded their trading activities either by closing their trades or being forced to exit due to stop orders being triggered. This occurrence leads to a consequential movement of the price further in the same direction, subsequently resulting in amplified financial losses.

Crypto-Based Mechanisms For Generating Passive Income

Ilalocating idle cryptocurrency assets for the purpose of earning interest serves as a highly effective means to generate returns on your invested capital. In the year 2022, we present a comprehensive compilation of six highly remunerative means through which one can generate passive income from the realm of cryptocurrency.

Passive income is derived when an individual is not actively engaged in the pursuit of business activities. A customary approach or platform for cryptocurrency investment involves allocating capital or digital assets to it, and subsequently awaiting a yield on one's investment. In certain instances, profits have the potential to be stable and consistent. Different situations may involve the influence of diverse and immeasurable forces that are beyond one's control.

A significant number of individuals invest in and retain cryptocurrencies with the intention of generating passive income, employing a strategy commonly referred to as "HODLing" within the cryptocurrency community. Investors are prepared to acquire a digital asset, basing their decision on the belief that its value will experience a substantial increase in the foreseeable future. This enduring strategy may necessitate investors to retain their positions for a duration of up to five years, nonetheless, these investors exhibit determination and perseverance. This investment does not require active engagement in the cryptocurrency market. After procuring the digital asset, they simply need to securely store it in a wallet that remains inaccessible to them.

In order to obtain access to your cryptocurrency, it is necessary to possess a wallet, which may take the form of either hardware or software. The non-custodial options allow for the storage of the private key on personal devices such as a computer, mobile phone, or dedicated wallet. This provides you with complete authority over your private keys and, ultimately, your digital assets. By contrast, a custodial wallet refers to a situation where the management of your private keys is entrusted to a third party.

Nevertheless, procuring and retaining a cryptocurrency asset over a prolonged duration does not guarantee financial gain. Undoubtedly, there is a high probability that you will incur financial losses. Merely engaging in the practice of retaining cryptocurrency holdings does not qualify as a genuine source of passive income.

Approaches to generating passive cryptocurrency income through Proof-of-Stake (PoS) staking

Proof-of-stake serves as a consensus mechanism utilized by blockchain networks, facilitating the agreement among distributed participants to incorporate up-to-date data into the blockchain. Significantly, blockchains facilitate open and decentralized networks wherein participants actively contribute to the governance and validation procedures of transactions. This holds immense significance as a community-focused approach eliminates the need for central institutions, such as banks. In general, blockchains usually employ a random selection process to designate participants as validators, subsequently rewarding them for their contributions.

The methodologies employed to designate validators diverge across different blockchain networks. Certain blockchain networks mandate that users provide a deposit or engage in a financial commitment towards the functioning of the network. The blockchain subsequently designates validators as individuals who have staked a specific quantity of the native digital asset. Validators are incentivized through the financial contributions they make, as a means to guarantee the integrity of the network. The process of verification is referred to as proof-of-stake. Consequently, long-term investors stand to gain from a consistent flow of revenue.

Take into account the utilization of PoS blockchains, wherein you can opt to entrust your stakes to other participants willing to assume the technical obligations of staking, since transaction validation could prove challenging. There are no unexpected revelations regarding the fact that validators receive higher compensation than delegators. Here is a list of Proof-of-Stake blockchains that deserve attention:

Cardano
Ethereum 2.0
Polkadot
Solana

Furthermore, you may consider employing one of the myriad staking services currently available. Using these platforms, it is possible to deposit a portion of the digital assets stipulated by the blockchain. In order to participate as a validator in the Ethereum 2.0 network, it is generally required to make a minimum deposit of 32 ETH or higher. One can potentially initiate interest accumulation with a minimal amount of 5 Ethereum by leveraging an Ethereum staking service.

Accounts that generate interest through digital assets

Investors can generate a consistent income from their dormant digital assets by utilizing interest-bearing crypto accounts. Consider it as depositing funds into a savings account that yields interest. The sole distinguishing factor of this business lies in its exclusive acceptance of bitcoin as the sole mode of payment. If you have a preference for not retaining your digital assets in wallets, these accounts provide you with the opportunity to consistently deposit them and generate income at predetermined rates. The subsequent entities are counted among the cryptocurrency service companies providing such products:

Nexo
Network Celsius

SwissBorg
BlockFi

Lending

Lending has witnessed a surge in popularity within both the centralized and decentralized realms of the cryptocurrency economy. It is conceivable to generate income through the practice of loaning your digital assets to individuals as an investor. You have four main options when it comes to loan strategies:

Peer-to-peer lending platforms offer users the ability to establish their own conditions, specify the desired loan amount, and set the interest rate at which they seek to earn returns. Similar to how peer-to-peer trade networks facilitate connections between buyers and sellers, the platform serves as a means of connecting lenders and borrowers. Through these lending solutions, customers are afforded a degree of agency with respect to their cryptocurrency loans. Nevertheless, it is essential that you initially transfer your digital asset into the custodial wallet provided by the loan platform.

The sole means of financing for this approach is the lending infrastructure provided by external parties. In this scenario, the interest rates and lock-up periods are both firmly established. In order to obtain income from the peer-to-peer lending platform, it is necessary to initially transfer your cryptocurrency assets to the lending platform.

Decentralized lending, also known as DeFi lending, facilitates direct lending transactions on the blockchain. In contrast to peer-to-peer and centralized lending models, decentralized finance (DeFi) lending operates without the need for intermediaries. Instead of that, lenders and borrowers engage through programmable and self-executing contracts (commonly referred to as smart contracts), which autonomously and periodically establish interest rates.

Ultimately, it is possible for you to authorize the loaning of your cryptographic assets to individuals who are actively seeking to engage in trading activities while utilizing borrowed funds. These traders utilize borrowed funds to augment their trading position and subsequently reimburse the loans with the addition of interest. In the present case, it is the cryptocurrency exchanges that primarily undertake the majority of the tasks on your behalf. You simply need to ensure that your digital asset is accessible for others to utilize.

Cloud mining

Certain blockchains, like Bitcoin, employ a more computationally intensive approach in which users must prove their eligibility as validators (commonly known as miners) through a competitive process of solving intricate mathematical puzzles. Cryptocurrency mining is the designated terminology for this particular undertaking. Competition within this consensus mechanism necessitates miners to incur substantial expenditures on advanced computational devices and bear exorbitant electricity costs.

This endeavor will require a significant amount of dedication and an extensive time commitment to bring to fruition. The surge in popularity of cloud mining can be attributed to this prevailing trend. By employing this approach, you can remunerate external entities to manage the technical aspects of cryptocurrency mining on your behalf. To put it differently, you would make a singular payment to a platform that provides these services in return for the lease or purchase of mining equipment from the platform's mining facilities. The requirement to pay a daily fee for the ongoing management of your mining rigs may vary depending on the cloud mining service provider you select subsequent to your initial payment.

There are manifold perils associated with this, notwithstanding its apparent allure. The issue of cloud mining has been a topic of discussion since it gained widespread recognition. Frauds directed towards this mining company have been prevalent due to its remote geographical location. Exercise caution while making this decision.

What are the reasons for engaging in Bitcoin mining?

Effective and innovative resolution

By electing to engage in Bitcoin mining with a well-regarded and long-standing enterprise like Genesis Mining, you will have the privilege of participating in their highly effective and exceptional approach that has consistently yielded positive outcomes throughout the years.

Many of the Bitcoin mining operations that are currently occurring are situated in heavily saturated Bitcoin farm markets. The utilization of potent, dedicated GPUs with programmable chips in the direct extraction of Bitcoins guarantees a seamless functioning mechanism that offers advantages to all involved parties.

Lucrative process of mining cryptocurrencies

Investors who commit substantial capital to endeavors like Bitcoin mining do so with the expectation of not only recouping their initial investment, but also generating a substantial long-term income. Such an outcome can be achieved through the utilization of Genesis Mining. Genesis, being a prominent Bitcoin mining company, possesses the proficiency to generate Bitcoins at an accelerated pace, thereby ensuring equitable financial gains for all pool participants who partake in the accrued profits.

Favorable encounters in the extraction of Bitcoins

You have the opportunity to join a highly regarded company that operates with exceptional efficiency in its systems and structures. In the beginning, the process of Bitcoin mining entailed considerable challenges such as computer malfunctions and exorbitant electricity expenses, among other issues. All of these challenges have subsequently been dealt with.

Concurrently engaging in the mining of both Bitcoins and altcoins "

It is crucial to acknowledge that both Bitcoins and altcoins can be mined simultaneously utilizing state-of-the-art hardware and software. If, for instance, you have an interest in mining Bitcoins, you have the option to engage exclusively in this activity. Nevertheless, should you have the inclination to partake in the extraction of alternative cryptocurrencies like LiteCoin and Ethereum, it is indeed a feasible endeavor.

Bitcoin remains a widely sought-after digital currency, enjoying significant global acceptance. It continues to uphold its decentralized nature, as it is generated through a collective community effort without the oversight of any central authority, central banking institution, or governmental entities.

All individuals have the liberty to become part of this community and engage in the purchase, utilization, and trade of Bitcoins. The cost associated with transferring Bitcoins between individuals or accounts is negligible. As a trader, you have the ability to engage in the trading, selling, purchasing, and receipt of Bitcoins. This highlights the remarkable versatility of Bitcoin. Nevertheless, there are constraints in place regarding the maximum quantity of Bitcoins that can be generated.

Bitcoin is created electronically and stored in virtual environments. It differs from other currencies such as the dollar, Euro, yen, pound, and others. Bitcoins are obtained or generated through the utilization of a network of interconnected computers that depend on specialized software and hardware. There exist numerous factors contributing to the widespread adoration of Bitcoin, which will likely persist as its usage endures over time.

By becoming a member of a reputable platform like Genesis Mining, you will establish a collaborative relationship with a proficient group of professionals who will provide guidance and guarantee your participation in the generated profits. Numerous accomplished investors have become part of the Genesis Mining community. Upon enrollment, you will be eligible for various bonuses and discounts. For more detailed information regarding Bitcoin mining, please refer to Genesis at

1
Foundational Principles of Trading

What precisely is trading?
Exchange of goods and services is an essential economic principle that involves the acquisition and disposition of assets. These can encompass goods or services for which the purchaser compensates the vendor. Under different

circumstances, the transaction may involve the mutual exchange of goods and services between the parties involved.

Financial instruments are assets that are exchanged within the realm of financial markets. These encompass various asset classes such as stocks, fixed income securities, currency pairs in the Forex market, derivative instruments like options and futures, leveraged products, digital currencies, and various other financial instruments. There is no need for concern if you lack familiarity with these phrases; we will comprehensively cover them in the subsequent sections of this post. The practice of engaging in brief trading activities, wherein traders actively initiate and exit positions within relatively condensed time spans, is commonly denoted as trading.

Nonetheless, this assumption is somewhat inaccurate. Indeed, the realm of trading encompasses a diverse array of strategies, including but not limited to day trading, swing trading, trend trading, and various others. But don't worry. We will examine each of these aspects more thoroughly at a later point.

What is investing?
Investment entails the allocation of various resources, notably capital, with the aim of generating a financial gain. This may entail the deployment of financial resources to provide backing and commence a venture, or acquiring real estate with the intention of subsequently selling it at a higher value. In the realm of financial markets, this frequently entails making investments in financial instruments with the objective of subsequently selling them at a higher price.

The underlying principle of investment revolves around the expectation of a return, commonly referred to as Return on Investment (ROI). In contrast to trading, investment frequently employs a more extended-term strategy in achieving wealth accumulation. The primary objective of an investor is to generate long-term financial growth and accumulation of wealth, which may span significant periods of time, encompassing years or even decades. There exist a multitude of approaches to accomplish this objective; however, investors frequently employ fundamental attributes in order to discern potentially advantageous investment prospects.

Investors typically do not concern themselves with short-term price fluctuations as they maintain a long-term perspective. Therefore, they will frequently maintain a state of passivity, exhibiting minimal concern towards immediate setbacks.

Trading vs. Discerning the disparity between investments.

Both traders and investors strive to generate profits within the realm of financial markets. Their methods for attaining this objective, nevertheless, display notable disparities. Typically, investors strive to generate a long-term financial gain, spanning several years or even several decades. Given the extended time frame of investors, their desired returns for individual investments also tend to be more substantial.

In contrast, traders seek to capitalize on the fluctuations present in the market. They engage in more frequent position entries and exits, and may seek lower returns per trade (due to their propensity for participating in multiple transactions). Which one is better? Which option aligns more favorably with your preferences? It is within your purview to make that determination. One can commence acquiring knowledge about the financial markets, subsequently honing their skills through practical application. Over the course of time, you will acquire the capacity to ascertain which option aligns more effectively with your financial objectives, personal disposition, and trading profile.

What does the term 'fundamental analysis' refer to?
Fundamental analysis involves the evaluation of a financial asset's worth or value. A core aspect of a financial

analyst's role involves thoroughly examining economic and financial factors in order to determine the validity of an item's value. These factors may encompass macroeconomic conditions such as the overall state of the economy, industry dynamics, or the specific business associated with the asset, if applicable. These indicators are typically monitored within the field of macroeconomics, both in terms of leading and lagging measurements.

After concluding the fundamental investigation, specialists strive to determine whether the asset is underestimated or overestimated. Investors can leverage this conclusion in their investment decision-making process.

In regards to cryptocurrencies, fundamental analysis can also encompass a burgeoning field of data science that delves into public blockchain data known as on-chain metrics. These indicators encompass the network hash rate, the most prominent beneficiaries, the quantity of addresses, examination of transactions, and various other factors. By utilizing the abundance of accessible data pertaining to public blockchains, specialists can formulate intricate technical indicators to assess diverse facets of the network's overall functionality.

Although fundamental analysis is widely utilized in the stock market or Forex, it is less suitable for cryptocurrencies in their present condition. This particular asset category is of recent origin, as a result of which a universally accepted and exhaustive approach for assessing market values has yet to be established. Additionally, a significant portion of the market is influenced by speculative practices and prevailing narratives. Consequently, the impact of basic variables on the price of a cryptocurrency tends to be minimal. Nevertheless, as the market progresses, it is plausible that more refined methodologies for assessing the value of cryptocurrency assets will emerge.

What does technical analysis (TA) entail?

Technical analysts employ a distinct methodology in their work. The fundamental premise underlying technical analysis lies in the notion that past price movements possess the potential to provide insight into future market behavior. Technical analysts do not aim to determine the fundamental value of an asset. Alternatively, they examine the past trading patterns and endeavor to identify potential opportunities based on that information. This may encompass an analysis of price fluctuations and trading volumes, examination of various chart patterns, utilization of technical indicators, and a wide array of charting instruments. The objective of this research is to assess the market's level of strength or vulnerability.

Having stated that, it should be noted that technical analysis is not merely a means of conjecturing potential future price movements. It also serves as a viable framework for effectively managing risks. Given its capacity to provide a framework for assessing market structure, technical analysis aids in establishing more precise and quantifiable transaction management. In this context, the initial measure towards effectively managing risk involves the quantification thereof. Consequently, certain technical analysts may not be exclusively considered as traders. They might employ technical analysis solely as a framework for managing risk. The utilization of technical analysis is applicable to various financial markets and is frequently utilized by cryptocurrency traders. However, does technical analysis yield effective results? As previously mentioned, the valuation of cryptocurrency markets is primarily driven by speculative activity. This provides technical analysts with a superb platform, as they can thrive solely by assessing technical matters.

Cryptocurrency Mining

What is the significance of mining?

Prior to the addition of a new block to the blockchain, it is imperative that the block, record, or transaction undergoes thorough confirmation and verification. The act of confirmation and verification is accomplished via the process of mining. Therefore, the need for miners in relation to blockchain-based cryptocurrencies such as bitcoin is constantly present. Miners are granted a reward each time they successfully solve and mine a new block, which comes in the form of a transaction fee. In the absence of miners, the addition of new records or blocks to the blockchain will be hindered, consequently impeding any transactional activities. There exist various methodologies for extracting cryptocurrencies. Let us examine each of them individually:

The various methodologies employed to extract cryptocurrencies

☐ Computational extraction

You have the ability to engage in computer-based mining. For instance, you can procure the software application known as GUIMiner, participate in a mining consortium, and commence the process of cryptocurrency extraction, specifically bitcoins, utilizing your personal computer. Nevertheless, a standalone computer lacks the sufficient computational capabilities to effectively mine a substantial quantity of cryptocurrency. It is highly likely that your electricity expenses would surpass the value of the cryptocurrency you could potentially mine. However, if your sole objective is to gain firsthand experience in the process of mining cryptocurrencies and are willing to overlook the minimal potential for earnings, then engaging in computer mining can be deemed as an auspicious initiation. When engaging in computer mining, exercise caution regarding the risk of overheating. It is advised to abstain from prolonged mining sessions as it may lead to the overheating and potential damage of your computer. Adhere to a predetermined timetable and ensure to allocate sufficient time for your computer to undergo the cooling process. If one is genuinely committed to generating considerable profits, it is advisable to contemplate the acquisition of hardware, which subsequently brings us to the subsequent form of mining referred to as hardware mining.

⬚ Mining through the use of physical hardware

In view of the limited mining potential of a stand-alone computer, it may be advisable to engage in hardware mining in order to secure a more substantial quantity of cryptocurrency. When utilizing hardware mining, your mining efforts will involve the utilization of both your computer and dedicated mining hardware. By utilizing this approach, you will experience an increase in mining potency, thereby enabling the acquisition of a greater number of cryptocurrencies. Once more, exercise caution regarding the matter of overheating. It is imperative to adhere to a predetermined schedule and grant your computer and hardware adequate time to cool off. One disadvantage associated with the utilization of hardware mining is the considerable cost that is often incurred when investing in high-quality mining equipment. It may require a considerable amount of time before you can recoup your investment in procuring a hardware.

Software extraction" or "Software data extraction

This mining approach entails the installation of software onto your computer in order to engage in the process of cryptocurrency mining. Typically, it would be expected that you acquire it through a commercial entity. The software provider also offers the possibility to upgrade your account in order to conduct mining operations for additional cryptocurrencies. Naturally, an extra charge is frequently levied for the purpose of enhancing your account or software. Furthermore, given your continued utilization of the computer, it is imperative that you remain vigilant of potential overheating issues, and it remains incumbent upon you to personally engage in the activity of mining cryptocurrencies.

Cloud-based mining

Cloud mining has emerged as the predominant approach for mining in contemporary times. With the implementation of cloud mining, computer utilization and concerns regarding overheating are rendered obsolete. However, the process entails merely awaiting the delivery of cryptocurrencies by a mining company. Typically, such deliveries occur on a weekly or monthly basis or whenever the minimum threshold amount is reached.

Naturally, it is not within the purview of any mining enterprise to dispense cryptocurrencies solely on the basis of benevolence. The essential aspect to consider is that an initial investment is required to be made in the form of a payment to the mining company. Below is an example of an offer: By investing 0.5 bitcoins, you have the potential to receive a weekly return of up to 0.008 bitcoins. While it may appear to be a satisfactory proposition, the issue lies in the fact that the figures presented by the mining company are likely to represent the projected yield rather than the actual sum you will receive. Prior to making any monetary deposits or investments, it is imperative that you thoroughly review and comprehend the terms and conditions. It is highly recommended that you also evaluate the feedback and reviews attributed to the cloud mining company. To retrieve feedback on a cloud mining company such as Genesis Mining, kindly employ your preferred web browser and enter the company name along with the term "reviews." The SERP will subsequently furnish you with pertinent webpages. Please peruse the evaluations and juxtapose them against the assessments attributed to other companies engaged in cloud mining.

Important observation: While there exists the potential for profitable returns through cryptocurrency mining, it is widely recommended by industry experts that those seeking substantial profits should focus their efforts on acquiring knowledge and skills in cryptocurrency trading and/or investment. An inherent drawback of mining operations lies in their limited profit potential, exacerbated by the likelihood of encountering various challenges such as overheating, substantial investments in hardware and software, and other unforeseen obstacles. Additionally, it should be noted that there exists a considerable number of fraudulent individuals who solely seek to defraud you of your financial resources. However, should you possess a genuine desire to engage in cryptocurrency mining, it remains a viable avenue for potential profit.

5: Blockchain

Blockchain can trace its origins to the advent of bitcoin; however, it has expanded its technological applications significantly, notably in the realm of cryptocurrency.

What is Blockchain?

According to the 2016 publication 'Blockchain Revolution' by Don and Alex Tapscott, blockchain is referred to as an unmodifiable electronic registry of economic transactions. They emphasize that its application extends beyond the realm of financial transactions and could be employed to register any valuable information through programming.

Comprehending the concept of blockchain may require some initial investment of time and mental effort. First and foremost, it is of utmost significance to note that it does not constitute a centralized repository of corporate information. However, it is a concept that endures indefinitely across a multitude of interconnected computational devices.

It undergoes regular updates and reconciliations, which are concurrently performed across the entire network. Alternative methods of record maintenance involve the dissemination of modifications made to a primary record to ensure the synchronization with other users. Due to its simultaneous presence across multiple locations and its ability to provide instantaneous updates to all connected parties, it is invulnerable to any form of corruption. Engaging in such an action would entail targeting each individual user simultaneously.

An alternative depiction of blockchain, most straightforward in nature, is to envision it as a colossal spreadsheet that undergoes discovery and simultaneous updates across multiple locations.

The data stored on a blockchain is accessible to a wide audience and can be verified through various sources utilizing the network. It is accessible to all individuals who are connected to the internet.

The analogy of a whistle blower can facilitate a deeper comprehension of the concept at hand. Consider a scenario in which an individual with characteristics similar to Edward Snowden has obtained unauthorized access to classified information. In the case of Snowden, he disseminated those classified documents among a select cohort of individuals in order to render the information more impervious to rebuttal. Blockchain extends its reach, allowing dissemination to anyone desiring access.

Nonetheless, a distinction arises when taking into account that the classified information was unearthed and initially retained by a solitary individual, namely, Snowden. Consider a scenario in which all individuals acquire knowledge of these secrets concurrently, and as each new revelation unfolds, universal awareness is instantaneously disseminated to all. The alteration of the existing collective knowledge is an unattainable feat.

Furthermore, one of the notable merits of Blockchain technology lies in its ability to undergo real-time updates. The addition of supplemental information to a file, subsequent transmission to another user, subsequent review and revision by said user, and subsequent return do not bear any logical consequence. No, in the case of Blockchain, updates are concurrently implemented for all users. Given the absence of an information relay system, there exists no juncture at which the data may be compromised.

That system possesses remarkable power and ensures a high degree of security.

How is money sent?

Cryptocurrency is stored within electronic wallets. Similar to a password, a Private Key grants the proprietor the ability to gain access to their assets. Additionally, every user is assigned a Public Key that serves to track the source and destination of the cryptocurrency.

Despite reports of individuals misplacing their private keys, resulting in the loss of their bitcoins' worth, it is crucial to note that these keys boast exceptionally high levels of security. The reason for this is that these entities are produced utilizing encryption technology, which generates codes that are nearly indecipherable.

What other factors contribute to its high level of security?

Due to the fact that the information stored on blockchain is consistently and uniformly accessed by all users, it gives rise to two notable advantages.

It is not under the control of any individual, institution, or organization.

It exhibits an unwavering performance across all fronts, owing to its constant online presence.

Moreover, given that each transaction is meticulously documented on every interconnected computer, a duplicated record is instantaneously generated and replicated across millions of instances.

This particular system exhibits a high degree of accountability and security.

Additionally, the system exhibits high levels of transparency as it undergoes updates at regular intervals of ten minutes, incorporating any transactions that have transpired since the previous update. These entities are commonly referred to as blocks, as they are intricately interconnected within the network, thereby forming the term 'blockchain'. These blocks are meticulously documented and firmly integrated within the network infrastructure. The sole means of altering the information entails the modification of the entirety of the network, and currently, there exist no computational systems possessing sufficient power to accomplish this task. In a pragmatic sense, the likelihood of such an outcome is exceedingly low.

Additionally, an additional security system that regulates itself is also in place. In contrast, while the act of robbing a bank results in the acquisition of currency that retains its intrinsic value, the act of 'stealing' bitcoins, for instance, would instantaneously render them devoid of value, given that they exclusively exist within the confines of the system and its records. It can be seen as a reverse catch 22 scenario, in which the only possible means of impeding Bitcoin transactions would require absolute control over each and every individual coin. However, this course of action would inevitably be widely acknowledged, leading to a collective refusal to recognize such transactions.

Nevertheless, it is not solely Bitcoin that benefits from the implementation of blockchain technology. The technology is applicable to every existing cryptocurrency, comprising hundreds, as well as any potential cryptocurrencies that may emerge in the future.

Additionally, it should be noted that although the details of transactions remain protected, the identity particulars of every user are always steadfast and unambiguous, characterized by their encrypted code. Their public key serves as an identifier of their identity. Distributed ledger systems, exemplified by blockchain technology, enhance the protection against identity theft and significantly raise the bar for falsifying identities.